ILLUSTRATED BY
GRACE HELMER

EDITED BY JOCELYN NORBURY
DESIGNED BY JACK CLUCAS
COVER DESIGN BY ANGIE ALLISON
WITH THANKS TO JONNY LEIGHTON

First published in Great Britain in 2018 by LOM ART, an imprint of
Michael O'Mara Books Limited, 9 Lion Yard, Tremadoc Road, London SW4 7NQ

W www.mombooks.com/lom
f Michael O'Mara Books
𝕏 @OMaraBooks
📷 @lomartbooks

A CIP catalogue record for this book is available from the British Library.

ISBN: 978-1-910552-88-9

2 4 6 8 10 9 7 5 3 1

Printed in July 2018 by Leo Paper Products Ltd, Heshan Astros
Printing Limited, Xuantan Temple Industrial Zone, Gulao
Town, Heshan City, Guangdong Province, China.

KAHLO'S KOALAS

1
PICASSO PANDA

2
KAHLO
KOALAS

3
LICHTENSTEIN
LLAMAS

4
MATISSE
MONKEYS

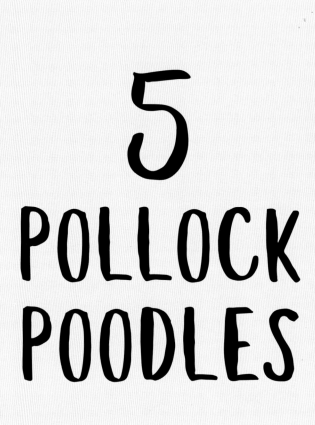

5
POLLOCK
POODLES

6
KANDINSKY KANGAROOS

7
VAN GOGH
GECKOS

8
SEURAT
SLOTHS

9
WARHOL
WARTHOGS

10
MONET
MICE

1 one

2 two

3 three

4 four

5 five

6 six

7 seven

8 eight

9 nine

10 ten

GALLERY OF ARTISTS

PABLO PICASSO
(1881 – 1973)

If Pablo Picasso had painted a panda, he would have used lots of unexpected shapes and colours. His painting would make you think you were looking at a panda from lots of different angles, all at once. This clever style is called Cubism.

FRIDA KAHLO
(1907 – 1954)

Frida Kahlo's paintings were inspired by her beautiful garden, her homeland of Mexico and her own fiery personality. If she had painted koalas, she would have been sure to feature her flowery headdresses and trademark dark eyebrows on the cuddly creatures.

ROY LICHTENSTEIN
(1923 – 1997)

Roy Lichtenstein's art bursts from the canvas like a 'Thwack!', 'Wham!' or 'Splat!' from a comic strip. His Pop Art paintings feature tongue-in-cheek scenes on top of dotty, colourful backgrounds.

HENRI MATISSE
(1869 – 1954)

Henri Matisse's cut-out collages are so full of joy that they seem to jump from the page and dance around the room. His bright, zesty images would have brought to life a troop of mischievous monkeys on the move.

JACKSON POLLOCK
(1912 – 1956)

Jackson Pollock knew how to make a splash. His paintings buzz with energy and combine drips, dribbles and splashes of paint. Pollock's style of 'action painting' is the perfect contrast to a prissy posse of parading poodles.

WASSILY KANDINSKY
(1866 – 1944)

Wassily Kandinsky combined strange shapes, dashing lines and daring colours. His images are described as 'abstract', which means they don't look exactly like the things we see in the real world. Instead, we fill the pictures with our own imagination and feelings.

VINCENT VAN GOGH
(1853 – 1890)

Swirling lines full of movement and life dash around Vincent van Gogh's paintings. It's easy to imagine he would draw geckos rushing and scrambling across the canvas. His wild and quickly-painted brushstrokes would be like colourful ripples flowing across a pond.

GEORGES SEURAT
(1859 – 1891)

Georges Seurat used teeny-tiny dots of colour to build up larger images. His work became known as Pointillism. Working like this was slow and painstaking, a bit like a sleepy sloth in the trees, moving from branch to branch.

ANDY WARHOL
(1928 – 1987)

Andy Warhol loved to make lots of prints of the same picture in a rainbow of different colours. But if he had painted a warthog, surely he couldn't have resisted showing it from the back as well as the front!

CLAUDE MONET
(1840 – 1926)

Claude Monet painted dreamy scenes full of waterlilies drifting across pretty ponds. His work was called Impressionism, and gave the impression or feeling of light and moving objects floating gently across the canvas.